**Slow
Burner**

Slow Burner
Fiona Sinclair

Smokestack Books
1 Lake Terrace,
Grewelthorpe,
Ripon HG4 3BU
e-mail: info@smokestack-books.co.uk
www.smokestack-books.co.uk

Text copyright 2018,
Fiona Sinclair,
all rights reserved.

ISBN 9781999827649

Smokestack Books
is represented
by Inpress Ltd

Contents

Time Travellers' Picnic	9
Crashing with Buddy Holly	10
A Game of Hide and Seek	11
Careless Talk	12
All in the Mind	13
Muscle Man	14
Bedside Manners	15
The Loved One	16
How to Milk a Snake	17
The Reluctant Bride and Groom	18
The Visitor	20
Women of a Certain Age	21
Absent Friends	22
Drama Lesson	23
Love Struck	24
Class of '76	26
Three's a Crowd…	27
The Artful Craftsman	28
Miss Nesbit	29
Last Respects	31
Leaving Highwood	33
Mystery Man	35

Time Travellers' Picnic

The guide book tempts with other Roman ruins.
We blow last lire on a hire car.
Leave sun beds and high street
where pushy traders hawk fake goods
with goblin market menace.
Bear picnic ingredients pilfered from hotel buffet.

I step into amphitheatre, utter genuine OMG,
no ruin but working order still.
My gaze track shots the full auditorium,
stone seating reaching O2 height and capacity.
In breath at cheap seat bonus, Taros mountains in distance.
Spotting imperial chaise lounge fashioned in marble,
awaiting cushions and reclining dignitary, giggle.
But the 'stage building' has me on the back foot,
fabulous façade time plundered,
it seals off the theatres semi-circle
like a wall of titanic bouncers.

You spot the roman stadium from the highway,
Sweeney skid to halt, abandon car in makeshift layby.
Looking down on the perfect horseshoe,
your eyes gleam as if seeing Anfield for the first time,
Remains and road are post-apocalyptic empty,
except for lizards cocking heads at us
as we clamber over rock fall masonry
lugging food in sports direct bag to reach intact seating.
I use my palm as plate to make jam sandwiches
whilst you with sportsman's eyes trace the track's
impression beneath the grass.
Suddenly, two Adhan like territorial cuckoos,
call out from either end of the valley, the day's final gift.

Crashing with Buddy Holly

A wintry walk shod in boots with bald tyre's tread,
Buddy Holly on Walkman you did not see
the ice snickering with slap stick intentions,
pavement's punch awaking the disorder like a sleeping curse.

Your symptom's alien language clumsily translated to GP as
Can't walk, pins and needles, numbness,
after glockenspiel play on elbows and knees…
doctor's diagnosis: *Well you've been through a lot lately.*

In the library your trembling fingers slid down columns
in medical dictionaries stopping ominous as a Ouija board
at MS ME MND, your heart amplified to a stethoscope roar as
you scanned symptoms which on paper seemed a perfect match.

Wheedling your GP for a third opinion with another consultant
who after a 10 minute examination, *I can find nothing wrong with you.*
Why can't I walk properly? Answered with a shrug.
Nevertheless relief unclenching you like a first gin and tonic.

Months on the symptoms slowly subdued leaving you
lacking the muscle now to queue for the Next sale
but managing to command a classroom perched on a table;
unaware that the fifth column affliction still sabotaged your body…

A Game of Hide and Seek

Her last chip, this London hospital,
clinical records given the slip somewhere in Kent,
a scribbled note from her GP, she sat before this consultant
with a new-born's medical history.
Lottery numbers excitement as he nodded at her narrative,
flourish of his fountain pen and she was entombed
in an MRI machine.
When her tight lipped body foiled his lines of enquiry
I think we'll keep an eye on you,
knowing some disorders play a game of hide and seek.
Writing degree essays in the waiting room
gave way to marking kid's homework
as check-ups routinely reassured her
I don't think there's anything to worry about.
So for years she didn't.

Careless Talk

The tests were routine as a leg wax now,
no greeting from the male medics chatting like Saturday girls,
Data will appear here, the dozing machine opens its eye, blinks twice,
student following his mentor's actions with the awe of a Dr Who assistant.

Hitch your skirt up, you curse the pubic hairs
self-seeded down your inner thigh,
but seeing the men momentarily freeze in DVD pause,
inwardly chuckle at capturing their full attention.

ECG gecko pads affixed to your legs, silence,
as the current twitches sinews in a mini *Mr Universe* display,
then a bolt deep into muscles that jump at each electrical bite,
gripping the couch you hold onto lemon cake at *Café Valerie* afterwards.

There's a significant change there, do you see?
Student's pen sprints across the pages of his notebook,
a sudden lift drop in your stomach,
exiting senior medic tosses over his shoulder

Your consultant will discuss the results with you,
anticipating a death row wait of weeks,
an ambulance siren in your head *I need to know now,*
instead you shuffle to the hospital entrance shackled by fear.

All in the Mind

Any family history of mental illness?
I can offer no great aunt teaming tweeds with straight jacket,
or uncle lurking in the lingerie section of M & S,
but shrugged *mum was an alcoholic,*
aunt's depression keeps turning up like a bad penny...
A line of stick figures conga across the psychiatrist's notepad.
After his questions empty the contents of my past like a dustbin,
He urges a leap of faith across my disbelief to his diagnosis.
Later I keep to myself internet research that *somatic*
was only recently divorced from its shady coupling with *psycho.*
Nevertheless explanation to friends
about a leaky mind contaminating its body
still met with a change of subject;
far easier to wear the fashionable label of bi-polar.

Muscle Man

Her fears frozen with permafrost local anaesthetic,
she grinned as the specialist rolled up his sleeves,
plunged a medical cheese tester into her thigh,
then knee against bed for purchase, tugged.

No breath held for results, knowing this branch of medicine
calliper limped towards any kind of cure, instead she planned
to have purple tyres on her wheelchair and a compartment for gin.

I can find no evidence of muscular disease. Destitute of next moves,
some relief when he suggested a colleague, but at *neuro-psychiatrist,*
she stared as if he had told an obscene joke, You *think this is
psychosomatic?*

He translated complex medical ideas into fact sheet simplicity,
overwhelmed brains could sometimes take it out on their own bodies.
Homeward it didn't occur to her to cancel thoughts of stair lifts and
hospices…

Bedside Manners

Whilst he read a copy of *The Lady*, you hid your eyes from
a young woman toddler tottering to the loo,
the man whose disobedient hands spilt tea.

Well it's good news from our point of view.
10 years of baffled shrugs, suddenly during a courtesy check up
a medic spotted something out of the corner of his eye.

Sound track to a disaster movie, you began to question…
but each *We don't know* revealed the specialist to be ignorant
of your condition as an 18th century saw bones.

At your whispered *Will I end up in a wheelchair?*
the consultant's smirked *Oh I think you are over-egging there,*
unintelligible to you as Latin.

In the nearest pub, your friend gulped red wine
gabbling about stem cell technology,
you downed a large gin, examined the doctor's words,

but finding only a few tight-lipped phrases,
unknown disease, no treatment,
you delivered your own dark prognosis.

The Loved One

No sooner spotted in the *Sunday Express*,
than the sports car bowled up outside the house.
In summer the saucy 60's glamour of taking its top off,
mother tying her headscarf a la Audrey Hepburn,
speeding around Kentish lanes in search of the Riviera.

After father's death, no money for new clutch, insurance…
but its disposal unthinkable as selling a child.
Locked in its garage until a rich man or pools win turned up
she bolted into the house if you partially raised the sliding door
for crooked back access to dustbins.
Occasional 'How does it look?'
you lied about the hood's mossy pelt, the sunken tyres…

When cancer began to feast on mother,
Triumph Spitfire needs attention in the local rag,
drew eager boy racers, mid-life crisis men,
who caressed the scarlet bodywork,
thrust themselves into the dainty seats,
groped beneath the bonnet.

Mother took to her bed with a bottle
whilst you played car dealer,
but entering her room clasping £500,
you found her watching from behind nets,
the car towed away at cortege pace,
the look on her face far worse than cancer's gnaw.

How to Milk a Snake

It was your grandmother played into uncle's hands,
sending him down each evening to 'do the garden',
after cancer had consumed your dad.

Mum, knowing his catalogue model looks
had captured both your grandmother and aunts' hearts,
forced to listen each evening to his obscene suit.

You became her body guard. Deadlock in the kitchen
as uncle must censor his speech,
his small talk finally running dry in the early hours.

His 'I want a woman who turns heads' to your aunt,
like detonating a dirty bomb, pitching the family into civil war,
the only solution, you and mum exiled 50 miles away.

In her new life's solitary confinement,
she listened, gulping wine, to his nightly sex chat calls,
milking him £40 a week for the service.

Eventually he sloped off to singles nights, remarried,
meantime mum had met the lodger,
a man who demanded more for his money.

The Reluctant Bride and Groom

He waited all summer for some other glittering girl
to catch his mate's attention,
then sidled up in tatty teddy boy jacket,
stuttered as if asking a girl out for the first time.
She accepted, to remain in the rich boy's eye-line.

Knocking for him, she negotiated the furniture thicket
that comprised the shop's stock,
its lichen streaking her summer coat.
Gagging at fry-ups ossified on Georgian tables,
she declined father's tipsy gesture towards stained tea pot,
tried to engage mother turned to stone by a gorgon disease,
whilst her date in peep toed socks
shamefully scooped out sandwich remains from a shoe,
her need to laugh supressed like a fart.

But after too many Saturday evenings
listening to the light programme,
when he suggested 'Dreamland' the following week
she agreed with wallflower relief.
Soon weekends were football socials, cricket club tea rotas…
Friends catching marriage like measles
urged 'Your turn next'
but eyes were avoided, subject changed

Finally his mumbled 'I suppose we'd better get hitched',
her mother's counsel over cocoa,
You're nearly 30; you'll be left on the shelf.
So she accepted his proposal like a below reserve bid.
But every few months a tearful *I don't love him,*
her mother reacting as if cancelling a wedding
was like recalling a launched invasion.

Until one May afternoon she found herself conveyed in a car
that seemed to fly at a whip-cracked pace to the church,
where she spotted her bridegroom's panting arrival
after a cartoon sprint across fields,
chanted to herself the inverted vows *I don't, I don't, I don't.*

The Visitor

for Keith

You arrive for the weekend welcome as a mini heat wave.
Seeing you only twice a year now since your move to Manchester,
a split seconds pause at your mocha skin, black cherry eyes…
which knocking about together, made me blind to,
but that have driven several of my female friends to try and 'turn you'.

300 mile drive and you are fresh as if chauffeured by limo.
We bowl down to Folkestone for ice cream,
cockles and the WW1 arch.
Visiting on the cusp of an art festival, an illuminated sign on a roof,
Heaven is a place where nothing ever happens,
belly laughter as a 30 foot sea gull is towed by. *This always happens to us.*

Three seater sofa ordered in your visit's honour delayed,
you insist I take the only arm chair with a *Well you are 10 years older,*
recline on the floor as if it was a 19th century chaise longue.
My eyelids shutters closing on the day, you take yourself off for a
stroll round Canterbury, chat to a young barman over a nightcap.

Your visit coincides with the Hop festival I usually cold shoulder.
In the high street chavs and pit bulls have been replaced by
local bands, vintage stalls, Morris dancers…
We titter at adults sporting hop headgear but two lagers later,
I wear a Titania chaplet, you a Bacchus crown.

Sunday our activity binge catches up with us,
we yawn over a late breakfast. You still have an itinerary
of lunch and tea with family and friends before the drive north.
Hugs at the front door. You leave. I do the washing up, change the
bedding …
feeling as if I have suffered a mini bereavement.

Women of a Certain Age

In the shared taxi she has bagged the front seat
beside the Elvis pretty driver.
Reclines as if already on a sun lounger
When does his shift end? Which clubs does he go to?
Her voice says late 40s, Louboutin heeled,
he giggles like a bashful girl, claims *Little English*.
But she has key phrases and gestures expressive as deaf alphabet,
so they manage a slow dance chat all the way into Side.
Two weeks sleeping in the sun all day like a cat,
evenings accessorised with scotch and Marlboro,
she will out-gyrate the belly girls,
that night's young man tip-toeing from her room
at 6 am clutching a hundred lira tip.
So disembarking at our hotel first,
she smirks back at my silently smiled *You go girl*.

In a Side side street I am snared by
cheap eye brow threading.
As the young man cats cradles cotton,
You have beautiful eyes, Are they contacts?
Years since wolf whistles stopped,
I shed 25 years at his compliment.
Studying more than the shape of my eyebrows
he reads, middle aged, British, alone,
begins to offer a la carte services
I can lick your pussy; bang until you bleed…
takes my laughter behind hands as coy fan coquetry.
I lead him on with empty Yes' half believing,
despite this town's fake Rolex, Mulberrys…
his *I will not charge because you are pretty.*
But at his sudden *What time shall I come to your hotel tonight*?
I thrust 20 lira at him, escape with a savvy 50 year olds
bad cheque promise to call the number on his card later.
Scurry back to *You should not be allowed out alone.*

Absent Friends

In M&S, her *Look at this, Look at this, Look at this*,
curtails again my own attempts to browse.
I teeter on the edge of slapping her,
cool off in the men's department.
Repentant, bear half her packages to Costa Coffee
buy cappuccino and cake, because she *did the driving love.*

Nearby, a middle aged woman huddles over her Kindle,
carrier bags as cover in case stood up,
a second woman stoops to search her features for girlish traces,
speaks her name with question mark.
Their embrace brings a friendship back from the dead,
then chaotic questioning as they sit with beaming emoticon faces.

A thickening in my throat as I remember:
the man whose weekly calls bi-polar swung between suicide strategy
and stomach cramping wit, who no longer phones me,
the woman whose getaway van I drove beyond
the reach of a husband's fists who has Facebook defriended me,
because my slot machine life suddenly paid out the windfall of a husband …

These two women never quite trashed
youthful remembrance of hennaed hair and flares,
whereas I am an amnesiac memory that no prompts
of Dickens, handbags, Paris will revive.
So I wrestle with yawns as a screed of texts sent to a lover
are read to me once more by a rebound friend.

Drama Lesson

Wrapt in the world she is writing,
the others have grabbed the glamour jobs,

temperaments are unleashed like fighting dogs
as they embark on an anarchy of improvisation.

Bursting through the barbican of her concentration
she delivers the script to girls whose thoughts

quicken with movement straight into the action
of a fairly-tale familiar as their own lives.

Catching their kinetic fever, she attempts to maintain
order, defending her work from eye-watering criticism.

Sudden as a spell, she casts herself back into
the stillness of a writer's stone memorial,

leaving the rest of the class to disintegrate
into a chaos of egos until the bell goes.

She packs away Drama. Her chatter wiping
the surface of her mind, ready for Maths.

Love Struck

Chronic illness commits marriage and Florence
into *it will never happen* box, then you bob up like a reprieve,
hand me lap top, credit card *Book it*.
Weeks between are tallied with teased
Do you believe you're going yet?
But at the airport I anticipate freak weather,
in the plane I predict engine trouble,
on Pisa platform I expect rail strike.

Merchant Ivory lead me to expect
my breath would be taken away on sight,
instead we drag cases over pedestrian crossing
plunge into thoroughfares that echo Rome, Milan…
Strict mini break schedule, we aim first for 'David'
but find all streets usher us to the Duomo's presence.
Your globetrotter tribute *It's better than the Taj Mahal.*
We dervish twirl at other city 'finds' on way to
Michelangelo museum where my gaze climbs and climbs
the titan statue that upstages your *Will you marry me?*

Citizens, glamorous as their city, fashion police inspect us,
your Crombie, my fake fur coat passed with approving nods
until we strut the streets. Boldly by passing two hour queue at Uffizi
with tale of your 'bad heart'. Ushered through entry rope like VIPs,
tourists straining to identify us behind our Ray Bans.
Inside, I snub Raphael, blank Titian in a room to room search
for the Botticelli Venus, 20 minutes audience
in her Rita Hayworth presence, and I develop a girl crush.

Ponte Vecchio, we anticipate Bridge of Sighs but get drab,
your *Perhaps its better inside* cancelled by rows of blingy jewellers.
Compensated by *Best hot chocolate ever* so thick we toddler giggle
as you stand your spoon up in it like a joke shop trick.
Outside the Medici palace, you are not to be fooled
by another plain Jane building, but I insist sensing treasure .
Your grumbles about *more steps* becoming *Have a look at this,*
two hours ogling emblazoned ceilings, walls, floors…

Late afternoons, wanting the city to myself,
I persuade you, with tryst palpitations,
to rest your sight-seeing strained back with
Won't get lost, Over spend, Be long,
then pelt down pension stairs, into the streets' embrace,
where I two time you with Florence.

Class of '76

In the bar I lift G and T with shaking hands,
then slowly ascend stairs to the reunion room.
'Old Girls' shriek greet each other,
my face and name met by many
with blank expressions quickly masked by hug.
I too struggle with faces changed by cosmetic time,
mostly just recognise a name.

Facebook has tracked down a teacher
who calls us to order round the tea table.
Biographies are started but soon hijacked
by questions, talking over, laughter…
We get the gist that most of us left qualification poor.
Careers advice, a head shake to college,
You'd make an excellent sales girl dear
so Top Shop, Miss Selfridge, Snob…
marking time until marriage.

Some lives took flight though;
naughtiest girl has a nursing degree,
prettiest girl has a wealthy husband,
boldest girl has a demolition business in Australia.
I stage fright forget half my trophy cupboard 's achievements
deliver 40 years in one rushed breath to wall, table, carpet,
avoid Q and A session by hasty *You next* to my neighbour.

We cluster around last class photo.
I redden at my teenage self,
no trace yet of mother's corrective genes,
but my father in drag,
little wonder no boy waited at the school gates for me.
Afterwards, scuttling down high street
head bowed as if still behind that face,
men outside restaurant suddenly shower compliments
I straighten up, sashay back to my car.

Three's a Crowd…

Snarl up has spin wheel landed him
directly outside their coffee shop.
Wife and friend sitting ducks in the front window,
for his ready *Rabbit Rabbit* gesture,
but clarinet toots become jazz trumpet blasts,
until he shrugs as the traffic propels him on.

Eve succumbed to coffee walnut cake and mocha,
the women lament between mouthfuls *I've put on half a stone*
place faith in the latest diet craze like a gambler's new system.
Exchange bulletins; family, work, social.
Voices lowered, agony aunt each other's 'concerns'.
Then free-run between Tory cuts and sale bargains,
Hands to mouth *No* at top trumped gossip,
Laughter running through like *Margate* in sea side rock.

Sound of the kitchen door
he abandons Liverpool match,
to shoot into the kitchen as if baring urgent news,
she unpacks shopping whilst he comic skits the incident,
but back turned stacking tins her neck hair senses
something crouching behind his
You two lovers – only had eyes for each other.

The Artful Craftsman

Despite you upping the pace past siren stores,
I speed window shop. Spotting it, I tug your hand
like a strong dog on a lead, forcing you to backtrack.

A couture stationers, with elegantly dressed
window display ; accessorised pens, paper, pencils
in gorgeous turquoise design, beckons me in

where I coo at paper carousal table decorations, though
we have no dining table, beam at books to note fine wines
though after years necking gin we are teetotal, searching

amongst these in breathe Ponte Vecchio proximity prices,
for an affordable item, whilst your hands are locked
in pockets against *not value for money* gewgaws.

Elderly proprietor, Italian charms us into ante room
for demonstration of paper design alchemy.
We firework *Oh* and *Ah* as paints are flourished

onto surface of porridge thick glue. Rapunzel combs
create peacock, Pollock, Missoni pattern. Thick paper
laid, then peeled to reveal perfect imprint.

You inspect racks of wrapping, confirm that despite
each designs familial DNA, hand casting is random element
that like human faces, makes no 2 sheets the same.

The owner watchers me with CCTV stealth
as I pace the shop, fighting urge to binge buy,
goes to work on me deftly as he paints,

gold and purple pattern I paw is *Renaissance old,*
then the Medici gambit *For you an extra 10% off,*
I scrabble in my bag, surrender my credit card…

Miss Nesbit

Often before play we must pay her a visit,
bearing stale cake, suspect meat, milk on the turn.
I dawdled behind, hoping we'd not find her den
which seemed to come and go like Brigadoon,
but Jo had internal sat nav that always
lead us to the dilapidated dormobile.

My mother, Daily Mail indoctrinated,
toted up Miss Nesbit's men's trousers string belted,
Millet's tartan shirt, builders' boots
and hinted darkly at something worse
than food poisoning lurking behind
her offers to little girls of mildew biscuits.

But beckoning us to view another injured bird
pushed from nest by siblings with fratricide intensions,
she was Amazonian indifferent to the bare breasts
it nestled between. Afterwards we worked our way back
through the woods our giggles bubbling up through
hand clamped mouths, Did you see…?

When she pitched up at Jo's house
cadging tea, sugar, conversation,
her mother, who collected characters,
would welcome her in for coffee,
where in cut glass voice softened by Irish gentry lilt
she let slip: Sorbonne, multi-lingual, Bletchley.

Sometimes village youths came looking for fun,
she would panic room crouch in locked van,
hands over ears against hard rock drumming on vehicle's sides,
scrabbling for hold as they pitched the van
like some nightmare fair-ground ride,
their roaring raising phone calls for the police.

Most evenings spent at the vicarage
with cleric chum who enjoyed a drink too,
talking divinity and racing tips into the early hours,
then blind man's bluff lurching home across A2,
until one night luck bankrupt,
she was hit and run left as human road kill.

Fifty years on, estate's new owners are many times
removed from original aristo family;
noblesse oblige not in their contract's Ts and Cs,
they have fenced off the woodlands,
hammered in screaming signs;
No fly tipping, No trespassing, No eccentrics…

Last Respects

The few lines *We've left Highwood*, winded her.
After fifty years a flit to another 'Lodge' in the Midlands,
central heating, double glazing, the *girls* to keep an eye on them.

One last drive down laurel lined memory lane;
It's like Christmas for her coming up here, father
delivering his daughter from only childhood to a house full…

Now building's ivy beard trimmed, cottage garden de-tangled,
the house was already becoming a stranger,
Help yourself, permission from estate agent showing prospects around.

Habit pulled her through naked rooms to kitchen.
Formica cupboards, enough to make retro dealers salivate,
removed, but trelliswork where family photos bloomed,

left on walls, the pictures plucked though.
In here, ordeal of raucous family suppers for the little girl,
Their mother her minder against family's verbal rough and tumble.

Two steps to the sitting room voided now of
wood burning stove, travel memorabilia on walls,
coffee tables littered with correspondence.

An adult friendship with the parents; tea in dainty cups,
wrapt by mother's tall tales of gothic coincidence and slapstick mishaps
contradicted by husband in rich Lawrence Olivier voice.

Ducking under the back door into the garden reclaimed from
near neighbour wood. She and Jo hours in their virtual world
where giant pampass grass was a monstrous spider.

Double back down badger burrowed passages to room
previously clad with father's 1,000 books. She beamed
when trusted with a Hemmingway because *I know you will return.*

For years an invisible rope across bottom of stairs,
Use the loo down here, dear. Now tip toe trespassed up,
open mouth discovering their secret, caved in master bedroom roof.

In Jo's cabin boy quarters, no Whimsy menagerie to finger
with pick pocket itch, but spatial reasoning test, how camp bed
was fitted in for sleepovers they stomach cramp giggled through.

Leaving Highwood, she spotted beneath an ornamental garden seat,
the garland that hanging from door knocker used to greet guests,
hesitated to rehome, instead laid the wreath on the front door step.

Leaving Highwood

That last morning, it was business as usual,
except he was coaxed from monkish dressing gown
into smart day clothes by 8 am.
Down in the Formica kitchen, walls a photomontage
of family life glamorous as Tattler pages,
they drank tea from Wedgewood cups,
cold shouldering toast,
he tackling the Times crossword
she and daughters batting chit chat around.

Ten o' clock applying lipstick,
Come on old girl to herself like a stern friend,
knowing full well another winter without central heating,
creeping damp from collapsed bedroom ceiling
would see them both off.
Cue for the car to pull round to front door,
looking straight ahead as if walking a tightrope
he passed through diamond paned room,
where wall to wall book cases housed his 80 years reading.
She followed straightening a cushion, adjusting a curtain.

The tearing skin of leaving after 60 years, unthinkable,
therefore family had agreed to be anaesthetised by double think,
only going away for a few days to *give Mummy a break*.
So whilst he occupied with sorting spectacles, Sudoku, sweets,
she turned and waved with vivid smile,
remarking the wisteria beginning to colour on this
everyone's lottery fantasy cottage,
as the car pulled hearse slow down the narrow lane.

In the hall, the sisters keened for the family home,
then encouraging each other with *it's for the best,*
marshalled packing cases, black bags, boxes,
junked old throws, dried flowers, broken bric a brac
wincing at the prick of each item's memory,
but the bulk of furniture, china, childhood souvenirs were
itemised and packed with curatorial care to be transported
to well to do daughter's estate 200 miles away,
where best chum, grandkids, other Kentish expats,
prepared invitations and gossip welcome basket
for the couple, at Highwood Lodge reloaded.

Mystery Man

No pillow talk, rather he dozes tight lipped as a spy.
So she must catch what he lets slip in daily life,
ELO on the radio whilst they decorate
I saw them at The Albert Hall…
She repaints the same skirting,
fighting her need for who with? when?
settling for *What was the band like?*
After Jeff Lynne is reviewed,
Do you think we should paint the ceiling?
cueing *that's enough* to her firmly as putting
the lid back on his chocolates.

Occasionally his history ambushes him;
a road in Liverpool recognized after 30 years,
she holds her breath as his dramatic monologue unfolds,
route to his mate's funeral, a TT race casualty,
roll call of other biker mourners *Ogy, Tex, Spider*
a few thumbnail sketched; *Noddy, He was a nutter…*
no biker chicks mentioned but then
brothers, bikes, birds, the natural order, she gathers.

When I was married to: When I was inside…
sometimes sudden revelations slap shock her,
yet he is adamant as a lying child *I told you this…*
Nevertheless brief Q and A session permitted,
her questions answered as if she was the prying press,
then time up, back to work on his laptop.
But questions persist in her like weeds,
however much she tries to smother them.